Contents

Living in Germany

Anne Frank was born in Frankfurt, in Germany, on 12 June 1929. Her parents were called Otto and Edith. They already had a three-year-old girl, Margot.

The Frank family was **Jewish**. In 1933, when Anne was four, the **Nazis** took power in Germany. They hated Jews and passed many **laws** against them. The Franks left Germany.

Living in Holland

The Franks moved to Amsterdam in Holland. Otto Frank made money selling herbs and spices. Anne and Margot went to school, made many friends and had picnics at the seaside.

But the **Nazi** government decided to **invade** countries nearby. War started between Germany and the **Allies**. In 1940 the Nazis took over Holland. They passed **laws** against **Jews**.

In hiding

Otto tried to get the family away. It was too late, so he made a hiding place called the **annexe** in his offices. The entrance was hidden behind a bookcase.

The Franks and three other people moved into the annexe in July 1942. Anne was thirteen. They shared five small rooms, one toilet and a washbasin. Anne kept a diary.

The long wait

During the day people worked in the building. Everyone in the **annexe** had to be very quiet. A few of their friends brought them food in secret.

They stayed hidden for two years. On 6 June 1944 English and American soldiers landed in Europe. It was just before Anne's fifteenth birthday. The Franks hoped the war would soon end.

Capture

On 4 August 1944 the **Nazis** found the **annexe**. The Franks were sent to a Dutch **concentration camp**. On 3 September they were sent to Auschwitz camp in Poland.

The Nazis were using Auschwitz as a prison camp. Here they killed **Jews** by gassing them. Anne, Margot and Edith stayed together at first. They never saw Otto Frank again.

Last days

By now the Russians were marching into Poland. The Germans left Auschwitz and moved many prisoners to camps in Germany. Anne and Margot arrived at Belsen camp in October 1944.

Anne's mother died in Auschwitz on
5 January 1945. On 15 April 1945, the
British freed Belsen. Anne and Margot
were already dead of **typhus**. Otto was
the only survivor of the family.

Photographs

There are many ways we can find out about Anne Frank and life for **Jews** under **Nazi** rule. This photo shows Jews being made to scrub the streets.

Otto Frank took lots of photos of his family. Many of these have survived for us to look at today. This is a photo of Anne and Margot.

Written clues

Newspapers and documents from the time tell us how the **Nazis** came to power. Modern **historians** have written about this, using **evidence** from the time.

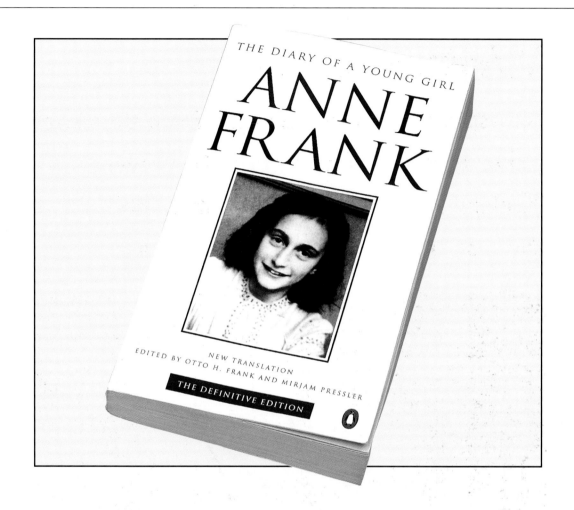

Anne wrote a diary while she was in the **annexe**. Some friends saved it and gave it to Otto after the war. Anne's diary tells us about her life in hiding.

House

The house in Amsterdam where Otto Frank had his office and built the secret **annexe** is still there. It is now a museum.

You can walk around the secret annexe. The photos of film stars that Anne stuck to the walls are still there. They are kept safe under glass.

Museums and exhibitions

The Anne Frank Foundation has **exhibitions** that show how the **Nazis** took power. They also show how people, before and after the Nazis, have treated **Jewish** people badly.

The Nazis destroyed most of the **concentration camps**. But one, Auschwitz in Poland, is now a museum. You can still see the huts where Anne and Margot were kept.

Glossary

This glossary explains difficult words and helps you to say words which may be hard to say.

Allies the armies of countries who fought against Germany during the Second World War. You say *Al-eyes*.

annexe part of a building that is separate from the rest of the building

concentration camp prison camp where people are kept because of their religion or race. You say *con-sen-tray-shun camp*.

evidence things which show us what happened, for example writing and photos

exhibition special display about a subject

historian person who studies and writes about the past

invade when an army goes into another country to take it over

Jew/Jewish person who is Jewish follows a religion called Judaism

law rule which tells people in a country what to do

Nazis the name of members of the German political party that took power in Germany in 1933. You say *Nat-zees*.

typhus illness caught by drinking dirty water. You say *tie-fuss*.

Index